Notes To Self

journal belongs to...

© 2016 Ranch House Press
All rights reserved. Printed in the United States of America.

www.annettebridges.com

ISBN: 978-1-946371-06-5

Journal Prompts
Notes To Self

This month's prompts are a list of "notes to self." You are invited to journal whatever comes to your mind that these "notes to self" inspire. And add your own notes to self in your journal!

1. I am doing the best I can with what I have in this moment. And that is all I can expect of anyone, including me!
2. Sometimes I have to forget what I want to remember what I deserve.
3. I can create my own happiness.
4. When I do what is best for me, I am also doing what is best for everyone.
5. When I eat like crap, I feel like crap.
6. What I think of me is more important than what other people think of me.
7. I am enough, I have enough and I do enough.
8. Read this BEFORE I do that again: DON'T DO THAT AGAIN!
9. Common sense is a flower that doesn't grow in everyone's garden.
10. I will work out, I will drink lots of water, I will consume green drinks daily, I will go to bed on time, I will repeat this over and over and eventually I will look hot in a bikini.
11. I am brave.
12. I'm going to make ME so proud.
13. I am not too old and it is not too late.
14. If I find myself constantly trying to prove my worth to someone, I have already forgotten my value.
15. Don't worry…if it's supposed to happen…it will.
16. Sometimes I have to remind myself that I don't have to do what everyone else is doing.
17. Leave the past in the past!
18. Finish each day and be done with it.
19. I don't have to take this day all at once, but rather one step, one breath, one moment at time. I am only one person. Things will get done when they get done.
20. RELAX!
21. I am allowed to cry, I am allowed to scream, but I am not allowed to give up. Breathe!
22. Don't chase people. Be me, do my own thing. The right people who belong in my life will come to me, and stay.
23. Stop forgetting I can have another reaction besides freaking out.
24. It's a good idea to ask, "What am I not doing?"
25. Before going to sleep every night forgive everyone and sleep with a clean heart.
26. Just because it pops into my head does NOT mean it should come out of my mouth.
27. Let people do what they need to do to make them happy. Mind my own business, and do what I need to do to make me happy.
28. Worry is a total waste of time. It doesn't change anything. All it does is steal my joy and keep me very busy doing nothing.
29. Let it go!
30. I am worth it!
31. Be there for others, but never leave myself behind.

color your world

ABOUT the CREATOR

Annette Bridges is an author, publisher and women's retreat host on a mission to help every woman realize her story is extraordinary, valuable and noteworthy.

She has published the *Color Your World Journal Series* and formed a journal club to provide community, support and tools for women to record their ideas, feelings, experiences, memories and all the important details of their lives.

Before writing books and publishing journals and coloring books, this former public school and homeschool educator spent a decade writing hundreds of helpful, instructive, and light-hearted columns published by Texas newspapers, parenting magazines, websites and bloggers.

Annette lives on a Texas cattle ranch with her husband John, dachshund Lady and lots of cows. She can drive a tractor but only if wearing a fresh coat of lipstick and it's not her pedicure day!

You can learn more about Annette's books and products, blogs and videos as well as her women's retreats and other events at www.annettebridges.com.

Look for her on social media, too!

MESSAGE from the PUBLISHER

The *Color Your World Journal Series* is a pathway to self-discovery. It's where you write notes to yourself. Be your own cheerleader. Give yourself encouragement. Tell yourself what you're grateful for. Celebrate you!

There are countless reasons to keep a journal including collecting favorite recipes, listing goals and celebrating every experience and every one that's near and dear to you. A journal provides a home for the memories and lessons learned that you never want to forget.

Why a niche journal?

If you're anything like me, you have a journal (or even two or three journals) where you write anything and everything about anything and everything. My challenge comes when trying to find something I've written. I flip and flip through the pages of my two, three or four journals trying to find whatever it is. I never remember which journal I wrote down my whatever's!!

The solution? A niche journal! A journal that has a specific focus and theme! A journal where you can record your ideas, inspirations and things you want to remember in the appropriate journal.

Why big unlined paper?

Because big unlined paper is needed to record big ideas, dreams and memories! You need room to grow, stretch and expand. You need space to think beyond the confines of what you've always done, to pursue new dreams, discover your power and reimagine your purpose again and again. You need pages without lines and limitations to reconnect with your creative, perfectly imperfect self.

Plus, big unlined paper gives you space for more than words. You have plenty of room to doodle, draw or post photographs and clippings, too.

Why color is important?

When you journal, use colored pens and markers! Your world doesn't happen in black and white. Your life should be lived and written about in many colors. Even dark and sad memories feel lighter and brighter when told in color.

Journaling in color affects your mood and perception of your world. Colors evoke calm, cheer and comfort. Using color can lift your spirit and inspire your imagination. You may be surprised by all the beautiful benefits from adding more color into your life story.

When journaling, give yourself time to listen to your heart and reflect. Breathe in the moments. Feel. Be quiet. Let yourself be totally and thoroughly present with your thoughts. Let your heart transform you and teach you new insights. Open your mind to consider new ideas and possibilities. You may find that what your heart teaches will be life changing.

www.ingramcontent.com/pod-product-compliance
Lightning Source LLC
Chambersburg PA
CBHW051253110526
44588CB00025B/2975